THE BAUHAUS PROJECT II: DESSAU

Tom Jacobson

BROADWAY PLAY PUBLISHING INC
New York
www.broadwayplaypublishing.com
info@broadwayplaypublishing.com

Cover photo by Francisco Hermosillo III

First edition: December 2024
I S B N: 979-8-88856-037-2

Book design: Marie Donovan
Page make-up: Adobe InDesign
Typeface: Palatino

THE BAUHAUS PROJECT II: DESSAU had its
world premiere on 20 July 2024 at Open Fist Theatre
Company in Los Angeles (produced by Martha
Demson & Amanda Weier with Associate Producer
Nychelle Hawk). The cast and creative contributors
were:

OWEN...Jack Goldwait
ELLIS ....Katarina Joy Lopez
KAI... John C Sweet
DUCK .... Sang Kim
BREC... Chloe Madriaga

Director ....Martha Demson
Assistant Director... Sarah Zuk
Stage Manager ....John Dimitri
Set design .... Richard Hoover
Lighting design .... Gavan Wyrick
Composer & sound design .... Tim Labor
Costume design ....Michael Mullen
Prop design .... Bruce Dickinson, Ina Shumaker
Projection design...Gabrieal Griego

CHARACTERS & SETTING

ELLIS, *20s-30s, theatre student, Southern accent, also plays:*
> FRITZ ERTL, *20s, student, carries a red book with a white spine*
> OTTI BERGER, *20s, textile instructor, Jewish*
> HANNES MEYER, *30s, architect*
> DANCER

BREC, *20s-30s, graphic design student, from Los Angeles, also plays:*
> GUNTA STÖLZL, *20s, weaving Master*
> HERBERT BAYER, *20s, graphic design instructor*
> LUDWIG MIES VAN DER ROHE, *40s, architect*
> MARCEL BREUER, *20s, furniture designer*
> HEINRICH PËUS, *50s, newspaper publisher*
> DANCER

KAI, *20s-30s, fine art student, from New York, also plays:*
> ARNOLD SCHÖNBERG, *50s, composer, Viennese accent, smokes cigarettes*
> OSKAR SCHLEMMER, *30s, painter, playwright, moves like a dancer*
> FRITZ HESSE, *40s, mayor of Dessau*

OWEN, *20s-30s, environmental design student, English accent, also plays:*
> WALTER GROPIUS, *30s, architect*
> PAUL KLEE, *40s, painter, Swiss accent*
> PAUL SCHULTZE-NAUMBURG, *50s, Nazi architect*

DUCK, *20s-30s, ESL music student, strong accent, also plays:*
>WASSILY KANDINSKY, *50s, painter, Russian accent*
>LÁSZLÓ MOHOLY-NAGY, *30s, photographer,*
>   *Hungarian accent*
>DANCER

The action takes place in an art school in Southern California in the present and in the Bauhaus in Dessau, Germany in the late 1920s to early 1930s. The only required scenic element is a modernist staircase.

SPECIAL THANKS

Josh Adams, Cyrus Alexander, Jonathan Bangs, Colin Bates, Bryan Bertone, Lou Danziger, Fran de Leon, Martha Demson, Presciliana Esperolini, Amanda Fekety, Éva Forgács, James Fowler, Ramón Garcia, Nychelle Hawk, Sarah Hollis, Jully Lee, Chelsea Kurtz, West Liang, Ramone Muñoz, Gary Patent, Kacie Rogers, Isabella Roland, David Shofner, Peter James Smith, Michael Sturgis, Donathan Walters and Dylan Wittrock

(Lights up on five students in their 20s or 30s: ELLIS, BREC, KAI, OWEN and DUCK. They speak to the audience. BREC is absent-mindedly carrying some kind of food. OWEN is wearing a button-down shirt and slacks and carrying a tablet or clipboard. DUCK is dressed conservatively with a touch of color, plus earbuds or headphones. KAI wears black.)

OWEN: *(English accent)* Thank you so much for joining us for our presentation on the *Staatliche Bauhaus*—

BREC: *(Hands on hips)* More commonly known in English simply as the Bauhaus—

OWEN: That isn't English—

DUCK: *(Heavy accent)*   ELLIS: It isn't even real
Cannot translate—   German—

KAI: *(New York accent)* This is our second presentation. Last term our assignment was the early years of the Bauhaus school of architecture and design from its founding in Weimar in 1919 to its closing there—

DUCK: By fucking   KAI & OWEN: —In 1925.
government!

(After an uncomfortable moment and perhaps an exchange of glares, OWEN continues.)

OWEN: This term we are presenting on the years the Bauhaus was in Dessau, Germany, 1925 through 1932. But first:

(Everyone looks to ELLIS, who steps forward, takes a moment, then:)

ELLIS: *(Southern accent)* We apologize to anyone—

ELLIS: —Who was offended—

BREC: Everyone!

ELLIS: —By our presentation last term. In our enthusiasm for the lessons of the Bauhaus and its relevance to our current political situation—

ELLIS: —We may have overreached—

DUCK: No fucking politic!

ELLIS: —In emphasizing—

BREC: Definitely overreached!

ELLIS: —The drama inherent in what seemed at first to us a straightforward story of art and design.

(ELLIS *steps back. Everyone stares at* ELLIS. *After a moment,* ELLIS *steps forward again, irritated.*)

ELLIS: I, in particular, apologize for my own additions to last term's presentation. My portrayal of—certain historical figures—was not—endorsed—

BREC: (*Taking a photo of* ELLIS) Not approved!

ELLIS: —By the full presentation team—

OWEN: Authorized!

ELLIS: —And I take responsibility for any discomfort my—

ELLIS: —Creativity—

BREC: Insensitivity!

ELLIS: —And improvisation—

KAI: Idiocy!

ELLIS: —May have caused. I found myself a bit— carried away—by the morality of design—

(*Seeing the others glaring,* ELLIS *steps back. They all continue to glare at* ELLIS, *who steps forward again.*)

ELLIS: We—

ELLIS: —Promise—

BREC: You!

ELLIS: That no such   OWEN: Commit!
improvisations—

ELLIS: —Or   BREC: Offenses!
interpolations—

ELLIS: —Will be a part of   KAI: Disruptions!
today's presentation.

(ELLIS *steps back and* OWEN *nods to* DUCK.)

DUCK: *(Looks at floor)* Presentation today is multi-discipline. Team represent many different department of school:

ELLIS: Theatre.

BREC: Graphics.

KAI: Fine art.

OWEN: Architecture.

DUCK: And music. Also, one change of cast from last term. Character of Fritz Ertl, last term play by me, this term play by:

(DUCK *looks at floor and gestures to* ELLIS *who smiles broadly and accepts the acknowledgment, perhaps even bowing slightly.)*

DUCK: Change necessary for—ah—fuck—you see!

ELLIS: Yes. We shall see.

OWEN: All other roles will continue from our last presentation, and a number of new historical characters will be introduced. We are retaining our narrative convention from last term despite a few difficulties—

ELLIS: Not just me, y'all!   OWEN: —With the narrator
                               role.

OWEN: Today we will have a series of three narrators, each a Director of the Bauhaus— *(Picks up rolled plans, indicates self)* Walter Gropius, Director from 1919 to 1928.

ELLIS: *(Dons pork-pie hat, indicates self)* Hannes Meyer, 1928 to 1930.

BREC: *(Dons long coat and indicates self)* And Ludwig Mies van der Rohe, Director from 1930 until 1933.

OWEN: Obviously a period of considerable disruption—

ELLIS: Conflict!   OWEN: —And change for the Bauhaus.

KAI: And Germany!

(All five make adjustments to their costumes, donning period attire.)

OWEN: Finally, a few bits of housekeeping and for transparency's sake, a word of disclosure and utter honesty:

KAI: Transparency?

(The others pause in their costuming, alarmed; this was not scripted.)

OWEN: This assignment last term and again this term is— *(Considers word choice)* Non-elective, and although I was instantly enthusiastic, not every member of our team expressed equal ardor for The Bauhaus Project at the outset.

KAI: With all due respect—

OWEN: *(Ploughing ahead)* However, as we researched and developed the second presentation, we all grew our appreciation of both history and each others' unique— *(Considers word choice)* —Gifts. I would like to thank my colleagues:

(Surprised and pleased, the others nod or otherwise acknowledge OWEN as their names are called.)

OWEN: Brec, Kai, Duck and Ellis for their commitment and talent. Brec for the program design, Kai for the art, Duck for original music and Ellis for direction—

ELLIS: *(Overlapping) Mise-en-scène!* I would just like to add… *(Pauses for effect and dread)* That another measure of an effective presentation is our ability to disappear into our characters—

OWEN: We're not   KAI: Transparency again.
actors—

ELLIS: —Empathizing with real individuals unlike ourselves and long dead and taking y'all along with us on the journey.

DUCK: And sure to like on the social media. I am apply to grad school.

KAI: Grad school?

ELLIS: *(Aggressively cheerful)* With my help!

OWEN: *(Pausing to make sure everyone is done)* And now, we are delighted to bring you *The Bauhaus Project II: Dessau.*

(OWEN *dons a hat and changes accent to become* WALTER GROPIUS *as the lights go out on everyone else.)*

OWEN AS GROPIUS: *(Gesturing with rolled plans)* *Wilkommen.* I am Walter Gropius, founder of the world-renowned Bauhaus school. Growing rapidly during our first six years in Weimar, the Bauhaus developed international fame for unornamented design in service of the people, mass production guided by artistic sensibility. Our modern ideas, while not in the least political, were such an inventive melding of art and craft that the state government of Thuringia, increasingly conservative, withdrew funding in 1925. Fortunately, the Bauhaus reputation made us attractive to a number of cities when we were forced out of Weimar, and we found a particular advocate in Fritz

Hesse, Lord Mayor of Dessau, best known until then for its Junkers aircraft plant.

(Lights up on KAI AS HESSE *giving a speech.* HESSE *has a low voice, a brimmed hat, a moustache and a cigar.* OWEN AS GROPIUS *observes, finger to temple.)*

KAI AS HESSE: Today, December 4, 1925, represents a great moment in the development of Dessau, transforming us from a modest residential town into a modern city of industry. By welcoming the distinguished Bauhaus school to our city, giving them asylum, I daresay, within the walls of Dessau, we will make the bells of all the arts ring again! You've already met Walter Gropius, founder of the Bauhaus and architect of the new Bauhaus complex at Dessau.

(Lights up on a wonderful utilitarian and modernist staircase.)

KAI AS HESSE: *(Gestures toward staircase)* The complex we inaugurate today embodies Bauhaus principles, a transparent architectural *gesamtkunstwerk*, a total work of art with a glass-covered workshop building, teaching facility and dormitory for twenty-eight students.

(Lights out on OWEN AS GROPIUS *and the staircase.)*

KAI AS HESSE: We are most honored to welcome the distinguished Russian abstract artist, Wassily Kandinsky, author of *Concerning the Spiritual in Art*, one of the most prominent members of the faculty.

(Lights up on DUCK AS KANDINSKY *with ramrod posture and a cardigan.)*

DUCK AS KANDINSKY: *(Russian accent)* My wife Nina and I look forward to move into new master house next year, but already I am happy with Bauhaus building. Exhibition space will show student art and sometimes maybe even paintings of those blessed to call ourselves artists, a term consider to some—how you say? —taboo at Bauhaus.

(Lights out on DUCK AS KANDINSKY *and up on* BREC AS STOLZL *who wears a headscarf and carries a sketchbook and a fabric sample.)*

KAI AS HESSE: Recently appointed the first female Master of the Bauhaus, Gunta Stolzl oversees the textile workshop.

(Lights out on KAI AS HESSE *and up slowly on* ELLIS AS ERTL, *who wears a burgundy Mazdaznan outfit and stands to the side, silent and disgruntled. He has tense, high shoulders and carries a book with a red cover and white spine.)*

BREC AS STOLZL: *(Precise pronunciation)* Our students— both male and female—are delighted by the six-storey dormitory with its gymnasium and showers. To call a friend, all they have to do is step onto their balconies and whistle. We aim for equality of the sexes, in social standing if not always in salaries for the Masters. *(Embarrassed, rushing)* But art is still the heart of what we do—not taboo at all! Our other most renowned artist, Paul Klee:

(Lights out on BREC AS STOLZL *and up on* OWEN AS KLEE, *who wears a bow tie and smokes a pipe.)*

OWEN AS KLEE: *(Swiss accent)* Perhaps not taboo, but I am concerned about the architectonic-constructive emphasis on utilitarian objects and the marketplace. What of absolute art, pure form, humanity itself—?!

(Lights up quickly on DUCK AS MOHOLY-NAGY *and out on* OWEN AS KLEE. MOHOLY-NAGY *wears glasses and a broad grin, carries a camera. His hair is parted in the middle.)*

DUCK AS MOHOLY-NAGY: *(Hungarian accent, manic)* Absolutely absolute art, Master Klee! Darling people of Dessau, I become Laszlo Moholy-Nagy from Budapest, new to faculty and pride to organize an education in famous Bauhaus introduction course. New building is crystal cathedral of arts as original describe in Bauhaus manifesto of 1919—which now we call The Bauhaus Idea—

(Lights up on KAI AS SCHLEMMER, *graceful and theatrical, with a tenor voice and mask pushed back on top of his head.)*

KAI AS SCHLEMMER: It seems the ultimate wisdom is compromise. The arts throughout Germany are shot down in their prime, victims of turbulent times—

DUCK AS MOHOLY-NAGY: Herr Schlemmer head up theatre program. Oskar, please tell us of that?

KAI AS SCHLEMMER: To eliminate pretension, our Bauhaus word is simply: stage. *(Gestures to room)* This stage, conveniently on the ground floor, is right next door to the lecture hall and cafeteria. The walls can disappear, a flexible innovation that allows us to combine all three into one large space. A literal form of architectural compromise—

DUCK AS MOHOLY-NAGY: Is not compromise! Is practical! Beautiful!

(Lights out on DUCK AS MOHOLY-NAGY *and* KAI AS SCHLEMMER *and up on* OWEN AS GROPIUS, *plans in hand.)*

OWEN AS GROPIUS: *(Finger to temple)* As you can see, there is considerable room within the Bauhaus Idea for disagreement, conflict, a wide range of opinions, but not politics. That dynamic atmosphere is healthy, not limiting, which is why we now describe the Bauhaus as an idea—

*(*ELLIS AS ERTL *begins to sing to the tune of* Deutschland Über Alles. *His voice is reminiscent of Peter Lorre.)*

ELLIS AS ERTL: *(Sings)*	OWEN AS GROPIUS:
Bauhaus, Bauhaus	—Larger than its constituent parts—

ELLIS AS ERTL: *(Sings)*   OWEN AS GROPIUS:
Über alles!   —Including music, yes,
                          of course, music!

ELLIS AS ERTL: *(Sings) Über alles in der Welt!*

OWEN AS GROPIUS: Our band is famous! As is the marvelously inventive Bauhaus dance!

*(*OWEN AS GROPIUS *gestures and delirious 1920s jazz dance music kicks in. Lights out on* OWEN AS GROPIUS *and up on* KAI AS SCHLEMMER, DUCK AS MOHOLY-NAGY *and* BREC AS STOLZL. *Along with* ELLIS AS ERTL, *they all begin to dance, everyone doing their own crazy, ecstatic gyrations. They stomp, buzz and fling themselves about, each in their own world. Soon they are joined by* OWEN AS KLEE *who does the wildest dance of all, making such a spectacle of himself that the others eventually all stop to watch until their lights fade out and he's left alone in spotlight. He freezes in a spectacular pose when the music ends. Lights out on* OWEN AS KLEE *and up on* DUCK AS MOHOLY-NAGY *and* ELLIS AS ERTL, *who carries his red book with a white spine. Before them is a board on which are mounted materials with a variety of textures.)*

ELLIS AS ERTL: *(Peter Lorre voice)* I don't understand.

DUCK AS MOHOLY-NAGY: *(Enthusiastic, joyful)* Excuse please: texture explore typical portion of introductory class, yes?

ELLIS AS ERTL: I have no idea what you just said.

DUCK AS MOHOLY-NAGY: When Itten teach, he also teach texture variance exercise? I continue tradition.

ELLIS AS ERTL: Master Itten taught the course in proper German.

DUCK AS MOHOLY-NAGY: I teach in Magyar! Language of the Steppes. *(Indicates objects)* Steppes of many texture, step by step I teach it, see? Tactility exercise most basic sensory experience!

ELLIS AS ERTL: There is no step-by-step of texture.

DUCK AS MOHOLY-NAGY: Excuse, please, but yes! *(Touching objects)* Supersmooth, very smooth, smooth, cross-hatched, abraided—

ELLIS AS ERTL: You're creating hierarchy where none exists!

DUCK AS MOHOLY-NAGY: Is better to teach! Tactile diagram—

ELLIS AS ERTL: The objects have meaning in and of themselves: *(Touching objects)* Vellum, fur, cardboard, plastic, wood, wax—

DUCK AS MOHOLY-NAGY: No, no! Must abstract! Is word in German, abstract?

ELLIS AS ERTL: Yes, we have the word abstract.

DUCK AS MOHOLY-NAGY: And constructivist!

ELLIS AS ERTL: That is not how Itten taught it! He invented the introductory course! And then Gropius forced him out!

DUCK AS MOHOLY-NAGY: For making spiritual samovars and intellectual doorknobs!

ELLIS AS ERTL: That was when Klee taught metallurgy! Not Itten!

DUCK AS MOHOLY-NAGY: You German not so good. You name, please?

ELLIS AS ERTL: Fritz Ertl.

DUCK AS MOHOLY-NAGY: Fritzi, I say it slow for you: Con-struc-ti-vist!

ELLIS AS ERTL: Don't call me Fritzi! I speak High German, not sucky German like you.

DUCK AS MOHOLY-NAGY: No suck! Invent!

ELLIS AS ERTL: Excuse, please.

DUCK AS MOHOLY-NAGY: Why you dress funny?

ELLIS AS ERTL: My religion! Also introduced by Master Itten. I am Mazdaznan.

DUCK AS MOHOLY-NAGY: Mazdaznan? I thought you Fritzi!

(Lights out on the confounded and mortified ELLIS AS ERTL *and up on* BREC AS BAYER, *a graphic design instructor who wears a vest, has a pencil moustache and carries a French curve.)*

DUCK AS MOHOLY-NAGY: Some students too—how you say? —conversative!

BREC AS BAYER: *(Soft-spoken, tenor, gentlemanly, with a warm smile)* They whine when I won't let them use Fraktur type. It holds Germany back, nationalistic and illegible.

DUCK AS MOHOLY-NAGY: You teach typography?

BREC AS BAYER: *(Shaking hands)* Herbert Bayer, still a student but soon to be a Junior Master, printing and advertising.

DUCK AS MOHOLY-NAGY: Typography must to be clear, otherthewise communication no good!

*(*DUCK AS MOHOLY-NAGY *shows a paper, which might be a projection of Fry's Electronics logo)*

DUCK AS MOHOLY-NAGY: Look: ugly cataclysm of form! Design by mental defective! Letter "s" a tragedy of Greek.

BREC AS BAYER: *(Agreeing)* The apostrophe turns it into an orphan. You could fit Russia between the "r" and the "y."

DUCK AS MOHOLY-NAGY: How do Germany recover from war with typeface from medieval time?

BREC AS BAYER: I'm working on a universalist sans serif typeface.

(BREC AS BAYER *shows* DUCK AS MOHOLY-NAGY *a piece of paper. The lower-case letters of the famous Bauhaus typeface may be projected.*)

DUCK AS MOHOLY-NAGY: (*Amazed and delighted*) No capital letters!

BREC AS BAYER: Why do we need capitals, a separate alphabet? We don't pronounce a capital A and a lower-case a.

DUCK AS MOHOLY-NAGY: Is better for mass production!

(*Lights out on* DUCK AS MOHOLY-NAGY.)

BREC AS BAYER: Beauty in utility.

(*Lights up on* KAI AS SCHLEMMER.)

KAI AS SCHLEMMER: May I use your typeface in the program for my Triadic Ballet?

BREC AS BAYER: Or all Bauhaus publications. An international revolution in print.

KAI AS SCHLEMMER: Don't let Gropius hear you say revolution!

BREC AS BAYER: Modernism is by its very nature progressive. That's why the National Socialists hate it.

KAI AS SCHLEMMER: Beauty in utility! I worry about reducing artists to intelligent house painters executing the orders of a higher necessity.

BREC AS BAYER: When I came to the Bauhaus, my ambition was to be a house painter.

KAI AS SCHLEMMER: No offense intended, Herr Bayer.

BREC AS BAYER: None taken. Now I think of myself as a form-giver. But your dance performances are hardly the work of a house painter.

KAI AS SCHLEMMER: I do paint, don't forget! And I'm starting to use photography in conjunction with my paintings, at least as a step in the process.

BREC AS BAYER: How?

(Lights out on BREC AS BAYER *and up on* ELLIS AS BERGER *on a staircase.* KAI AS SCHLEMMER *is photographing her.* BERGER *wears a cloche hat and has a Slavic [Yugoslavian] accent.)*

KAI AS SCHLEMMER: Go up!

*(*ELLIS AS BERGER *ascends a couple of stairs.)*

KAI AS SCHLEMMER: Now down.

(When she doesn't move)

KAI AS SCHLEMMER: Down please!

ELLIS AS BERGER: *(Slavic accent)* Sorry, I didn't hear you.

*(*ELLIS AS BERGER *turns and descends a few steps.)*

KAI AS SCHLEMMER: Must I shout?

ELLIS AS BERGER: Actually, yes, if I'm facing away. I'm a little deaf.

KAI AS SCHLEMMER: It looks better when you're facing away. Up again.

ELLIS AS BERGER: Thanks.

KAI AS SCHLEMMER: You're no less pretty from behind.

ELLIS AS BERGER: I'm working hard to construe that as a compliment.

KAI AS SCHLEMMER: Ultimately you won't be a woman, but an abstraction.

ELLIS AS BERGER: Nice!

KAI AS SCHLEMMER: Try the landing. And go *en pointe* like a dancer.

*(*ELLIS AS BERGER *tries to go en pointe, but loses balance.)*

ELLIS AS BERGER: I weave better than I dance.

KAI AS SCHLEMMER: Move to a different step.

(ELLIS AS BERGER *reluctantly moves to a different step. By the time* SCHLEMMER *finishes photographing her, she will have taken every pose in* SCHLEMMER'S *famous Bauhaus staircase painting.*)

KAI AS SCHLEMMER: Another. (*Louder*) Another! (*Photographs*) A few steps higher, please!!

ELLIS AS BERGER: Stop shouting at me!

KAI AS SCHLEMMER: I'm the director. Directors shout!

(BREC AS STOLZL *comes by carrying spools and skeins and eating something.*)

ELLIS AS BERGER: Oh, Gunta, thank God! Come model with me!

BREC AS STOLZL: Otti, I'm not ready for class!

KAI AS SCHLEMMER: Please, Gunta, just a few minutes! The non-objective relationship between people on the stairs is what interests me.

ELLIS AS BERGER: You're looking especially non-objective today.

(BREC AS STOLZL *drops what she's carrying and joins* ELLIS AS BERGER *on the stairs, sharing the snack.*)

BREC AS STOLZL: A few minutes only!

KAI AS SCHLEMMER: Away from me, please!

ELLIS AS BERGER: Oskar wants to photograph our asses.

KAI AS SCHLEMMER: To me they're nothing but slightly ovoid spheres! Look over the railing, please.

ELLIS AS BERGER: Your husband won't object, will he?

BREC AS STOLZL: We're not married yet. I can show my ass to anyone I please.

KAI AS SCHLEMMER: One go high and one go low.

(They comply.)

ELLIS AS BERGER: So unromantic for a woman almost wed. Us single girls must be more seductive. *(Poses seductively)*

KAI AS SCHLEMMER: Just walk up the stairs like a normal person.

*(*ELLIS AS BERGER *adjusts position.)*

BREC AS STOLZL: I'm trying some new threads today—synthetic.

*(*BREC AS STOLZL *and* ELLIS AS BERGER *strike an increasing wild series of poses.)*

ELLIS AS BERGER: Plastic?

BREC AS STOLZL: No!

ELLIS AS BERGER: I'm serious! Imagine the durability, the tactility! Fabric is best understood with the hands!

BREC AS STOLZL: You couldn't wear plastic.

ELLIS AS BERGER: I mean drapery or upholstery. I'm seeking a patent.

BREC AS STOLZL: A patent! For yourself or the Bauhaus?

ELLIS AS BERGER: It's my idea!

BREC AS STOLZL: Don't let Gropius find out!

ELLIS AS BERGER: And metallics. They're the story!

KAI AS SCHLEMMER: No talking! You're the most undisciplined models!

BREC AS STOLZL: We're not models, Oskar, we're artists!

KAI AS SCHLEMMER: Artists of the loom! Penelopes!

ELLIS AS BERGER: Weaving is not just for women!

BREC AS STOLZL: We're more than merely intelligent house painters!

KAI AS SCHLEMMER: Where'd you hear that?

BREC AS STOLZL: Herbert Bayer. We're very close.

KAI AS SCHLEMMER: That's enough, ladies, thank you.

ELLIS AS BERGER: It just got fun!

BREC AS STOLZL: Are you pouting, Oskar?

KAI AS SCHLEMMER: I'm not pouting!

(KAI AS SCHLEMMER *storms off.* ELLIS AS BERGER *helps* BREC AS STOLZL *gather up the spools and skeins.*)

ELLIS AS BERGER: I hope you don't speak to your Arieh that way.

BREC AS STOLZL: We have a very modern relationship.

ELLIS AS BERGER: Will he require you to keep kosher?

BREC AS STOLZL: He's barely religious.

ELLIS AS BERGER: Men sometimes surprise you with their expectations. My grandfather made my grandmother keep a kosher home in Zmajevac.

(DUCK AS KANDINSKY *appears in a painting smock.*)

BREC AS STOLZL: If I marry Arieh, I'll lose my German citizenship and become Palestinian by default.

DUCK AS KANDINSKY: Pardon me, frauleins. I just finish painting and no one there is to show it to. You would oblige me?

ELLIS AS BERGER: Master Kandinsky, we're late for the textile studio—

BREC AS STOLZL: How nice! Perhaps just a peek!

DUCK AS KANDINSKY: Then I must not to delay you—

ELLIS AS BERGER: Master Schlemmer took up our whole morning with modeling on the stairs!	BREC AS STOLZL: Oh, Otti, his studio's just around the corner—

ELLIS AS BERGER: DUCK AS KANDINSKY:
I can't hear a thing with   As you wish.
everyone talking at once!

ELLIS AS BERGER: I really should go. Good-bye, my dear.

BREC AS STOLZL: I'll see you in a few minutes, Otti!

(ELLIS AS BERGER *disappears.*)

DUCK AS KANDINSKY: Fraulein Berger is friend?

BREC AS STOLZL: We're colleagues in the weaving studio.

DUCK AS KANDINSKY: You know she is Jewess.

BREC AS STOLZL: Master Kandinsky, I may soon be Jewish myself, if I can ever find time to marry Arieh as he wishes.

DUCK AS KANDINSKY: Is that be wise these days?

BREC AS STOLZL: I know you're just looking out for me, which I appreciate…

DUCK AS KANDINSKY: I am last anti-Semitic person you ever meet. Arnold Schönberg is great friend. My color theories inspire his opera, *The Lucky Hand*—

BREC AS STOLZL: Oh, I know—

DUCK AS KANDINSKY: Also Marcel Breuer, Moholy-Nagy—

BREC AS STOLZL: They're Christian now—

DUCK AS KANDINSKY: Not Breuer, he consider to conversion so to marry—

BREC AS STOLZL: As am I, Master Kandinsky. Let's speak no more of it.

DUCK AS KANDINSKY: It is not Arieh Sharon's religion but his politics I object.

BREC AS STOLZL: It's his politics I admire, actually.

DUCK AS KANDINSKY: The Communists to destroy Germany, Europe!

BREC AS STOLZL: DUCK AS KANDINSKY:
He's a socialist!   Just as they did Russia!

BREC AS STOLZL: And I am, too.

DUCK AS KANDINSKY: Ah. Then, as you say, let us speak no more of it.

BREC AS STOLZL: Yes, let me see your painting.

DUCK AS KANDINSKY: Alas, we use up all our time in the talking. I must to clean myself before I teach.

(OWEN AS GROPIUS *appears, plans in hand, tries to pass them swiftly.*)

BREC AS STOLZL: Me, too! I'll see your painting after class, Master Kandinsky! Show the Director your work!

(BREC AS STOLZL *dashes out.*)

DUCK AS KANDINSKY: Gropius!

OWEN AS GROPIUS: *(Caught, finger to temple)* You have a new painting, Wassily?

DUCK AS KANDINSKY: Yes, come see, please.

OWEN AS GROPIUS: I would love to, but I've an appointment to make a dunning telephone call.

DUCK AS KANDINSKY: Dunning?

OWEN AS GROPIUS: A factory in Berlin has licensed Wilhelm's table lamp in prototype. Apparently they're already selling like mad before they've paid us a single mark.

DUCK AS KANDINSKY: This manufacture is problem! You rush to kiss anus of commerce but no time for art. Product workshops priority with painting in dust.

OWEN AS GROPIUS: I'll make the call then come see you.

DUCK AS KANDINSKY: Too soon I have class.

OWEN AS GROPIUS: Then later this evening—

DUCK AS KANDINSKY: This age is struggle between spiritual and material. My painting show so clear!

OWEN AS GROPIUS: Of course, Wassily, that's why I hired you—

DUCK AS KANDINSKY: No longer we say art but design. Not architecture but construction, not theatre but stage.

OWEN AS GROPIUS: An unpretentious vocabulary defines the Bauhaus Idea: the whole man, molded by humane design, which is the spirit.

DUCK AS KANDINSKY: Design for mass production, no individual expression.

OWEN AS GROPIUS: Germany must focus on efficiency of production to catch up with the rest of Europe. We bring beauty to production.

DUCK AS KANDINSKY: Then art is dead?

OWEN AS GROPIUS: No, it lives in every table lamp, every teacup, in the wallpaper!

DUCK AS KANDINSKY: Art must be useful?

OWEN AS GROPIUS: Master Schlemmer is creating a ballet of ideas. And music? Is that useful?

DUCK AS KANDINSKY: Is beauty only.

OWEN AS GROPIUS: Exactly, and at the Bauhaus we are devoted to music.

DUCK AS KANDINSKY: Music school in city is headless.

OWEN AS GROPIUS: But I've been thinking: could we invite your friend Arnold Schönberg to come direct the music school?

DUCK AS KANDINSKY: He would lunge at chance!

OWEN AS GROPIUS: Steady work and he could compose—

DUCK AS KANDINSKY:
Live with us here!

OWEN AS GROPIUS:
And influence German music even more than he has so far.

DUCK AS KANDINSKY: I write him! He is like brother!

(*Lights out on* DUCK AS KANDINSKY. OWEN AS GROPIUS *turns to the audience.*)

OWEN AS GROPIUS: With passionately opinionated Masters, conflicting goals, and the occasional conservative student, I had my hands full at the Dessau Bauhaus. But I never imagined my biggest challenge would be: a chair.

(*Lights up on a Wassily chair designed by Marcel Breuer.*)

OWEN AS GROPIUS: Inspired by tubular bicycle handles, Marcel Breuer turned to furniture design when he wasn't getting architectural commissions.

(BREC AS BREUER *appears and sits in the chair. He wears a blazer and carries a chrome pipe.*)

OWEN AS GROPIUS: There is no truth to the rumor that Breuer designed the club chair for Wassily Kandinsky.

(DUCK AS KANDINSKY *appears and sees* BREC AS BREUER *in the chair.*)

DUCK AS KANDINSKY: Is beauty only!

BREC AS BREUER: (*Slight Hungarian accent, baritone, energetic*) On the contrary, Master Kandinsky, it's a very practical chair designed for mass production. (*Showing him chrome pipe*) Note the tubular structure, cast without seams so it's strong as a bicycle, light to carry— (*Lifts the chair*) —But supports the body of an adult man.

(BREC AS BREUER *seats* DUCK AS KANDINSKY *in the chair.*)

DUCK AS KANDINSKY: Is very comfortable! What is called, please?

BREC AS BREUER: Model B3.

DUCK AS KANDINSKY: Name is not—how you say?—evocative.

OWEN AS GROPIUS: Decades later, an Italian design firm made this one of the most popular chairs in history, marketing it as the Wassily chair.

(Lights out on DUCK AS KANDINSKY *in the chair.* BREC AS BREUER *pulls a paper from his pocket.)*

OWEN AS GROPIUS: Breuer was an exceptional student, soon to become a Master, and I had my eye on him for my possible successor as Director of the Bauhaus. But I was unaware of his personal struggle.

BREC AS BREUER: *(Reads paper)* To the Official Provincial Rabbinate of Frankfurt, I, Marcel Lajos Breuer, do hereby declare that I no longer wish to be considered a Jew, and do renounce the religion of Judaism, committing to no future practice of its rituals, celebrations or regulations beginning this 22nd day of May, 1926.

OWEN AS GROPIUS: Ostensibly his renunciation was so he could marry his Bauhaus sweetheart, Marta Erps, but I suspected a more paranoid motivation that I judged an overreaction. At the time.

(Lights out on BREC AS BREUER.*)*

OWEN AS GROPIUS: My immediate concern was the chair—

*(*ELLIS AS ERTL *bursts in.)*

ELLIS AS ERTL: Herr Director, I wish to register a complaint.

OWEN AS GROPIUS: *(Fingers to temples)* Again, Fritz?

ELLIS AS ERTL: I've just learned of Gunta Stolzl's role in the departure of Johannes Itten from the Bauhaus.

OWEN AS GROPIUS: What role is that?

ELLIS AS ERTL: She betrayed him!

OWEN AS GROPIUS: To whom?

ELLIS AS ERTL: To you!

OWEN AS GROPIUS: Master Stolzl revealed nothing to me about Itten that was not already known.

ELLIS AS ERTL: Fraulein Stolzl's betrayal of a confidence is grounds for dismissal.

OWEN AS GROPIUS: Will that be all, Fritz?

ELLIS AS ERTL: I have a second complaint.

OWEN AS GROPIUS: Of course.

ELLIS AS ERTL: I was prevented by campus security from posting this.

(ELLIS AS ERTL *reveals a poster that says* Emil Evers für Oberbürgermeister der Stadt Dessau, *depicting a handsome 30-something man in a suit with a swastika armband.*)

OWEN AS GROPIUS: Herr Ertl, the Bauhaus is resolutely apolitical.

ELLIS AS ERTL: These are dangerous times. The need is urgent.

OWEN AS GROPIUS: Your candidate is running against Lord Mayor Hesse, our patron and champion of the Bauhaus.

ELLIS AS ERTL: Hesse has socialist leanings.

OWEN AS GROPIUS: You are campaigning against the Bauhaus itself, against your own self interest. Do you not understand that?

ELLIS AS ERTL: I am campaigning for the soul of Germany!

OWEN AS GROPIUS: *(Laughing)* Get out of here, Fritzi!

ELLIS AS ERTL: Don't call me Fritzi!

(Lights out on ELLIS AS ERTL.*)*

OWEN AS GROPIUS: Too late I realized what that laugh cost me.

(Lights out on OWEN AS GROPIUS *and up on* DUCK AS KANDINSKY *narrating a letter.)*

DUCK AS KANDINSKY: Dear friend: There are so many opportunities at the Bauhaus to start a fire at the center then radiate out to ignite the world. So often I say "if only Schönberg could be a part of this!" And now I have learned from confidential sources that there is a search for a new director of the music school here. If that position would be of interest to you, please write me immediately. Gropius and I can set right to work on it. Warmest regards to you and your family, yours always, Kandinsky.

(Lights out on DUCK AS KANDINSKY *and up on* KAI AS SCHÖNBERG, *smoking a cigarette and wearing a suitcoat. His eyes tend to bug out.)*

KAI AS SCHÖNBERG: *(Viennese accent)* Dear Herr Kandinsky: A year ago your letter would have summoned me straight to the Bauhaus, so great is my passion for teaching. However, I have finally learned the lesson Europe has forced upon me my whole life: I am not a German, not a European, perhaps not even a human being. I am a Jew and only a Jew. Moreover, I have learned that even Kandinsky agrees. Our friendship was but a dream. We are two different kinds of people, without a doubt. I send my most polite and respectful salutations to the Kandinsky I knew in the past and the Kandinsky of today. Schönberg.

(Lights out on KAI AS SCHÖNBERG *and up on* OWEN AS GROPIUS *and* ELLIS AS ERTL. OWEN AS GROPIUS *waves a*

newspaper at ELLIS AS ERTL, *who carries his red book with a white spine.)*

OWEN AS GROPIUS: Herr Ertl, are these caricatures yours?

ELLIS AS ERTL: Caricatures?

OWEN AS GROPIUS: Political cartoons in the *Dessauer Volksblatt.* Depictions of me!

(DUCK *appears, grabs hat from* OWEN AS GROPIUS, *puts it on and becomes* GROPIUS *in caricature.)*

DUCK AS GROPIUS: The family is a patriarchal system, an enslavement of women.

(KAI *appears, takes the hat from* DUCK, *puts it on, grabs rolled plans from* OWEN *and becomes* GROPIUS.)

KAI AS GROPIUS: Apartments must become machines for living in!

(OWEN *grabs back the hat and plans.* KAI *and* DUCK *disappear.)*

ELLIS AS ERTL: You actually said those things.

OWEN AS GROPIUS: So you admit it.

ELLIS AS ERTL: You said them publicly, Herr Director. Anyone could have told the publisher.

OWEN AS GROPIUS: *(Rattling the paper)* Who then wrote this editorial:

(*Lights up on* BREC AS PEUS, *a breezily smug publisher with a monocle and handlebar mustache.)*

BREC AS PEUS: *(Wrinkling nose in disgust)* Director Gropius proposes destruction of the German family. He is a socialist ceding all authority to the state, a collectivization of workers instead of mothers, fathers and children!

(*Lights out on* BREC AS PEUS.*)*

OWEN AS GROPIUS: I'm negotiating with Mayor Hesse to get university status for the Bauhaus, and this weakens my position.

ELLIS AS ERTL: I assure you I had nothing to do with the newspaper!

(Lights out on OWEN AS GROPIUS *and up on* KAI AS HESSE.)

ELLIS AS ERTL: Lord Mayor, I'm here as a tax-paying citizen as well as a concerned student.

KAI AS HESSE: You're Fritz Ertl, aren't you?

ELLIS AS ERTL: Yes. I'm flattered you've heard of me.

KAI AS HESSE: With all due respect, you're campaigning for Emil Evers, my opponent.

ELLIS AS ERTL: I feel it's my duty to report that Walter Gropius, Director of the Bauhaus, is derelict in his duties, spending his time on architectural projects here and in Berlin.

KAI AS HESSE: Herr Ertl, good day. Please leave my office and do not return.

ELLIS AS ERTL: Gropius is destroying the Bauhaus, firing the best instructors—

KAI AS HESSE: Good day!

(Lights out on ELLIS AS ERTL *and up on* OWEN AS GROPIUS.)

KAI AS HESSE: I'm doing my best to defend you.

OWEN AS GROPIUS: Against these newspaper attacks?

KAI AS HESSE: The town council, your own students! You mustn't get involved in politics!

OWEN AS GROPIUS: I care nothing for politics.

KAI AS HESSE: You spoke against motherhood of all things!

OWEN AS GROPIUS: I'm merely protecting myself and the Bauhaus. Ninety percent of our time is defending our reputation locally, nationally, internationally, and only ten percent on actual work!

KAI AS HESSE: Let me protect you. I've successfully negotiated university status for the school. You and the master teachers are now officially professors. Congratulations!

OWEN AS GROPIUS: Thank you, Lord Mayor!

KAI AS HESSE: But the council is proposing a cut to next year's budget.

OWEN AS GROPIUS: How much?

KAI AS HESSE: Ten percent. A greater cut next year if trends continue.

OWEN AS GROPIUS: We are starting to get many industrial orders, licensing furniture, tableware, architectural commissions—

KAI AS HESSE: Ah, yes, I know—

OWEN AS GROPIUS: But everyone it seems is a slow pay.

KAI AS HESSE: If the Bauhaus can become financially self-sustaining—

OWEN AS GROPIUS: Ten percent, I understand.

(*Lights out on* KAI AS HESSE *and up on* DUCK AS KANDINSKY.)

DUCK AS KANDINSKY: We always get the cream of the crap.

OWEN AS GROPIUS: It's temporary only.

DUCK AS KANDINSKY: I will not accept. Neither, Klee.

OWEN AS GROPIUS: All the other instructors are taking the pay cut. They're invested in the future of the Bauhaus.

DUCK AS KANDINSKY: The collective.

OWEN AS GROPIUS: We are all in this together,
yes. You've just been made full professors as you
requested.

DUCK AS KANDINSKY: For less pay.

OWEN AS GROPIUS: Temporarily!

DUCK AS KANDINSKY: It is trend. Painters disrespected.
Extreme specialization preventing synthesis.
Spirituality kaput! You never say art no more.

OWEN AS GROPIUS: I am committed to the highest
quality—

DUCK AS KANDINSKY: Quality, not art. Quality of fine
pickle jar, perfectly efficient teapot!

OWEN AS GROPIUS: Would you accept a five percent
cut?

(Lights out on OWEN AS GROPIUS. DUCK AS KANDINSKY
writes a letter.)

DUCK AS KANDINSKY: Dear Herr Schönberg: Your
letter shocked me to the core. I love you as an artist
and a friend; nationality is the least of my concerns.
Among my friends are many Jews, one since grammar
school. I would very much like to discuss with you
"the Jewish question." If you have heard—from what
sources I cannot imagine—that I made remarks you
find offensive, why did you not write me immediately?
I reject you as a Jew but think of you personally among
the supermen who rise above, the few who are human
beings, not Jews, Russians, Germans, Europeans. If you
choose to cut ties with me, I nevertheless send you my
kindest regards and highest esteem. Kandinsky.

(Lights out DUCK AS KANDINSKY *and up on* OWEN AS
GROPIUS.)*

OWEN AS GROPIUS: I, of course, had no notion of the painful correspondence between Kandinsky and Schönberg, preoccupied as I was with the accusations of Heinrich Peus and the *Dessauer Volksblatt*.

(Lights up on BREC AS PEUS.*)*

BREC AS PEUS: *(Wrinkles nose in disgust)* The people of Dessau have had enough of the excesses of your new architectural style. Flat roofs piled high with snow! What were you thinking?

OWEN AS GROPIUS: Flat roofs save thirty-three-point-eight percent of the costs of a traditional double tile roof.

BREC AS PEUS: *(Waddling away)* Academic journals and the German housing industry have published critiques.

OWEN AS GROPIUS: *(Following)* Which I have refuted in the Bauhaus journal.

BREC AS PEUS: A defensive posture, of course! But right-thinking Germans see through your theories, as I've pointed out in the *Volksblatt*.

OWEN AS GROPIUS: I've written a letter of rebuttal and demand you print it, along with a retraction.

BREC AS PEUS: *(Waddling away)* I have in fact, a new article with additional grievances already typeset and in page proof. It is too late and I am too busy to speak further today.

(Lights out on BREC AS PEUS *and up on* KAI AS HESSE.*)*

KAI AS HESSE: I cannot control the newspapers. This is Germany. We have a free press!

OWEN AS GROPIUS: These attacks come just as our finances are improving! Schwintzer and Gräff has licensed fifty-three different light fixture models, Rasch has made wallpaper our most profitable product, our typography is in demand for packages of cigarettes, chocolates, shoes!

KAI AS HESSE: And they are paying?

OWEN AS GROPIUS: Finally! And enrollment is booming! Prospective students at an all-time high, two hundred applications a week from all over the world!

KAI AS HESSE: I am most gratified to hear it.

OWEN AS GROPIUS: However?

KAI AS HESSE: You've been spending too much time in Berlin—

OWEN AS GROPIUS: It's my architectural commissions that kept us going until the industrial fees started coming in—

KAI AS HESSE: With all due respect, I need to ask you to deduct the Berlin time from your vacation.

OWEN AS GROPIUS: This is not coming from you.

KAI AS HESSE: I represent the council.

OWEN AS GROPIUS: I have been grooming Marcel Breuer as my successor—

KAI AS HESSE: No, Walter, don't talk like that—

OWEN AS GROPIUS: The *Volksblatt* attacked me personally, and now my wages are to be garnished—!

KAI AS HESSE: Your vacation—!

OWEN AS GROPIUS: Perhaps it's better for the Bauhaus to go on without me.

KAI AS HESSE: It can't go on without you! You're the founder!

(Lights out on KAI AS HESSE *and up on* BREC AS BREUER *and the club chair.)*

OWEN AS GROPIUS: It's taken forever, but at last we have a draft contract for marketing your club chair in Dresden.

BREC AS BREUER: Oh.

OWEN AS GROPIUS: You hardly seem overjoyed. I'm beside myself—a profound victory!

BREC AS BREUER: On my behalf you negotiated?

OWEN AS GROPIUS: On behalf of the Bauhaus. The club chairs will eclipse the wallpaper sales and we won't have to worry about funding from the Dessau town council.

BREC AS BREUER: The club chair is my intellectual property.

OWEN AS GROPIUS: You conceived and developed it as an employee of the Bauhaus.

BREC AS BREUER: I sold Standard-Möbel Lengyel Company manufacturing rights to the chair two weeks ago. My rights.

OWEN AS GROPIUS: I'm…astonished.

BREC AS BREUER: It's not a Bauhaus product. Is a painting by Klee a Bauhaus product?

OWEN AS GROPIUS: A chair is not a painting, as Kandinsky often reminds me.

BREC AS BREUER: I made it on my own time in my workshop.

OWEN AS GROPIUS: Perhaps this is why I've heard nothing in response to my letter.

BREC AS BREUER: Which letter?

OWEN AS GROPIUS: I circulated a letter among faculty asking for help with administrative tasks. I gave it first to Moholy-Nagy, who handed it to Muche, who gave it to you.

BREC AS BREUER: I've been busy.

OWEN AS GROPIUS: Busy negotiating with Standard-Möbel Lengyel Company! Marcel, my heart is breaking. Of all our students, you were the most talented. You've flourished as a Master, led the way. I had thought that when I left you might lead the Bauhaus.

BREC AS BREUER: When you leave—?!

OWEN AS GROPIUS: Apparently I need to revise my plan.

(Lights out on the chair, OWEN AS GROPIUS *and* BREC AS BREUER *and up on* KAI AS SCHÖNBERG *responding to* KANDINSKY's *letter.)*

KAI AS SCHÖNBERG: *(Smoking)* Dear Kandinsky: I am glad you were moved by my letter, but I see we still do not understand each other. When I walk down the street, with everyone looking to see whether I'm Jew or Christian, should I wear a placard like a blind beggar telling them I'm a Jew for whom Kandinsky makes an exception? Would such a placard persuade that man Hitler?

(Lights slowly come up on an agitated DUCK AS KANDINSKY *standing by* OWEN AS GROPIUS *who reads* SCHÖNBERG'S *letter. The rolled plans may be on a table or desk.)*

KAI AS SCHÖNBERG: Every summer for five years I've vacationed at Mattsee, a resort near Salzburg. This summer's peace was denied when they refused me entry as a Jew. And now you reject me as a Jew. As a communist, a warmonger for profit. Pseudo-science based on the libelous Protocols of the Elders of Zion. Kandinsky endorses this poison? Depriving Jews of their civil rights? That may rid the world of me, Einstein, Mahler, but you will not be able to exterminate a people who've survived unaided against the whole of mankind for twenty centuries. If we ever meet again, it would be sad for us to be blind to each other. Please pass on my cordial greetings to the Kandinsky I once knew. Schönberg.

(Lights out on KAI AS SCHÖNBERG. OWEN AS GROPIUS *puts down the letter.)*

OWEN AS GROPIUS: *(Fingers to temples)* This is Alma's doing.

DUCK AS KANDINSKY: How you know? You are divorce since 1921.

OWEN AS GROPIUS: Did you ever do anything to offend her?

DUCK AS KANDINSKY: What you mean? No!

OWEN AS GROPIUS: It could have been quite innocuous. She wears her passions on her skin.

DUCK AS KANDINSKY: She one time make—how you say?—pass after me.

OWEN AS GROPIUS: She makes a pass at everyone.

DUCK AS KANDINSKY: I tell her no, I am happily marry to Nina!

OWEN AS GROPIUS: Did you now?

DUCK AS KANDINSKY: I no sleep with you wife. She is like sex on assembly line, industrial erotics!

OWEN AS GROPIUS: That sounds like the voice of experience.

DUCK AS KANDINSKY: Gropius, I swear!

OWEN AS GROPIUS: I'm teasing you, Wassily! If you turned her down you were probably the only rejection of her entire life. No wonder she poisoned your relationship with Schönberg. *(Giggles)* Oh, you naughty Alma.

DUCK AS KANDINSKY: Is no funny.

OWEN AS GROPIUS: No one knows that better than I.

DUCK AS KANDINSKY: She tell everyone I am Bolshevik!

OWEN AS GROPIUS: Maybe you should have cuckolded me. *(Brandishing paper)* Do you read the *Dessauer Volksblatt?*

DUCK AS KANDINSKY: Sometime…

OWEN AS GROPIUS: I appear to be a daily feature on the editorial page.

DUCK AS KANDINSKY: Yes, I have seen.

OWEN AS GROPIUS: Wassily, you've been part of the Bauhaus since almost the beginning.

DUCK AS KANDINSKY: Six year.

OWEN AS GROPIUS: So perhaps you can explain to me why now—as we are finally moving toward financial stability—the spirit of the Bauhaus seems to have died.

DUCK AS KANDINSKY: Spirit? Died?

OWEN AS GROPIUS: When we started we were poor, everything was difficult, so everyone pitched in, made sacrifices for the Bauhaus Idea—

DUCK AS KANDINSKY: This is about another pay cut? I no consent!

OWEN AS GROPIUS: Your pay's restored. You're a full professor.

(Lights up slowly on the Wassily chair.)

OWEN AS GROPIUS: When I asked the Masters for administrative help, no one responded. *(Irritated when he notices the chair)* I assumed—quite wrongly, I realize—that what was designed at the Bauhaus belonged to the Bauhaus—

DUCK AS KANDINSKY: Not my paintings!

OWEN AS GROPIUS: Nor apparently, chairs, textiles, everyone's seeking their own patents, making secret deals with manufacturers—

DUCK AS KANDINSKY: Paintings not manufacture! Art!

OWEN AS GROPIUS: And now— *(Brandishes paper)* — When I'm pilloried daily in the paper, no one comes to my defense—not one letter to the editor from staff, faculty or student! I think of the Bauhaus as my family, but they've abandoned me for other ideas.

DUCK AS KANDINSKY: Some are Communists, some join National Socialists.

OWEN AS GROPIUS: Once I could balance the right and the left, but no more. Germany is more polarized than before the war!

DUCK AS KANDINSKY: I can but paint.

OWEN AS GROPIUS: Yes, please! Go make yourself more famous at our expense.

DUCK AS KANDINSKY: I make Bauhaus famous!

OWEN AS GROPIUS: Thank you, Wassily, for helping me decide. We no longer share a vision. It's time for me to leave the Bauhaus.

DUCK AS KANDINSKY: You are founder!

OWEN AS GROPIUS: A strong organization can survive the departure of its founder. Can the Bauhaus adapt as the world changes? The world has never been like this before.

DUCK AS KANDINSKY: Cannot adapt without you!

OWEN AS GROPIUS: If I'd known in 1919 I'd only have nine years to build this—experiment—of the Bauhaus, I wouldn't have tried. What's happened to the Bauhaus Idea? What's happened to us?

DUCK AS KANDINSKY: Gropius is Bauhaus!

OWEN AS GROPIUS: Do you think Hannes Meyer would be a good choice for the next Director?

DUCK AS KANDINSKY: Hannes Mayer?!

(Lights out on them and the chair. In the darkness, strange music, perhaps by Schönberg or Hindemith. Lights up on KAI AS SCHLEMMER, *narrating a dance performance.)*

KAI AS SCHLEMMER: Theatre serves the metaphysical needs of man by creating a transcendental world of illusion on a rational basis.

(Lights come up on a DANCER *in a strange, geometric costume in a yellow set. The dancer dances.)*

KAI AS SCHLEMMER: Ideally, dancers should not have faces. We only want to see their bodies in space—their geometry is what is beautiful. Puppets and marionettes are superior, more abstract, but masks and costumes can transform the human body into something more aesthetically pleasing than flesh: a figurine.

*(*DANCER *continues dancing. The movements are greatly restricted by the costume.)*

KAI AS SCHLEMMER: The Triadic Ballet is in three parts, with three dancers. The first act is yellow, cheerful, burlesque.

(After a few moments, OWEN AS GROPIUS *appears in separate light.)*

OWEN AS GROPIUS: *(Finger to temple)* Dear Sir: After considerable thought, I have made a decision to leave this sphere of activity and request a meeting to discuss early termination of my contract.

(Another DANCER *joins the first, in a similarly geometric costume. They acknowledge each other as they dance but do not touch. Lighting change.)*

KAI AS SCHLEMMER: The second act is pink, celebratory but sober. The modern world is divided into the mechanical *(man as machine)* and primitive creative urges which come from within. The geometry of dance synthesizes the two.

*(*DANCERS *dance.* OWEN AS GROPIUS *is intrigued by the dance, proud of it, a bit distracted from his letter.)*

OWEN AS GROPIUS: As my own architecture practice has grown, I find myself more and more often away from Dessau. The Bauhaus has also grown, a child now able to walk and even run on its own. I can leave without detriment.

(A third DANCER *joins the other two. Similar geometric costume. Lighting change.)*

KAI AS SCHLEMMER: The third act is black, mystical and fantastical. The Dionysian abandon of primordial dance governed by strict Apollonian symmetries.

(Dance continues. A light slowly comes up on the Wassily chair.)

OWEN AS GROPIUS: I plan, in collaboration with my former colleagues—who have been very close to me both professionally and personally—to spread the Bauhaus Idea via broader applications in Germany and throughout the world, including my own architectural work.

(Dance continues. OWEN AS GROPIUS *notices the Wassily chair with some annoyance. Is it mocking him?)*

KAI AS SCHLEMMER: The greatest virtue of Baroque theatre is silence. When the word is silent, the body alone is articulate and free.

*(*OWEN AS GROPIUS *watches in silence for a few moments as the* DANCERS *dance.)*

OWEN AS GROPIUS: For my successor I propose the head of our architecture department, personally and professionally qualified to lead the institution to further accomplishment: Professor Hannes Meyer.

(DANCERS *freeze, may quickly remove masks in order to say:)*

DANCERS & KAI AS SCHLEMMER: Hannes Meyer?!

OWEN AS GROPIUS: *(To the audience)* Professor Meyer will not only become the new Director of the Bauhaus, but he will also— *(Starts choking up)* —Apologies—also take over as your narrator in just a few minutes. Thank you…for allowing me the privilege of serving…

DANCERS & KAI AS SCHLEMMER: Hannes Meyer!?!?

(Overcome, OWEN AS GROPIUS *flees and nearly trips over the Wassily chair. The rolled architectural plans go flying.)*

OWEN AS GROPIUS: Goddamn chair!

*(*OWEN AS GROPIUS *leaves. Lighting change puts the chair in darkness.* HANNES MEYER, *played by* ELLIS, *gives a speech.* MEYER *wears a jaunty pork-pie hat and carries the rolled architectural plans previously carried by* GROPIUS.)*

ELLIS AS MEYER: *(Swiss accent) Gruëzi* [hello]! I am Hannes Meyer, as of today, April 1, 1928, the new Director of the Bauhaus. And your narrator for the rest of this presentation.

*(*DUCK AS MOHOLY-NAGY, BREC AS BAYER, KAI AS SCHLEMMER *and* OWEN AS KLEE *appear, listening to the speech.)*

ELLIS AS MEYER: By way of introduction and to give you an idea of my plans for the future of the Bauhaus, I've constructed a poem, a new manifesto, actually, entitled *Bauhaus and Society. (Reads)*
The Bauhaus at Dessau is not an artistic endeavor
But a social revolution.
We give birth to form,

But society is the midwife.
Our work is determined by society.

(*Some consternation among* DUCK AS MOHOLY-NAGY,
BREC AS BAYER, KAI AS SCHLEMMER *and* OWEN AS KLEE.)

ELLIS AS MEYER: The modern German people require
A thousand schools, parks and public buildings,
A million home furnishings,
So it's our duty
To put the needs of the people first.

(BREC AS BAYER *bids the others farewell [perhaps shaking
hands] and disappears.)*

ELLIS AS MEYER: The aim of life is pursuit of harmony
Which we call growth,
The urge toward harmonious processing of
Oxygen, carbon, sugar, starch and protein
Which we call work.

(*Perhaps showing a bit more exasperation than* BAYER,
DUCK AS MOHOLY-NAGY *makes his departure.*)

ELLIS AS MEYER: We are not striving to create
A Bauhaus style or Bauhaus fashion.

(KAI AS SCHLEMMER *takes his somewhat theatrical leave, on
his way out bumping into* BREC AS BREUER, *who has come
to see what's going on.*)

ELLIS AS MEYER: We reject formalism.
The goal of all things Bauhaus
Is the merging of generative forces
For a harmonic society.

(*Having seen enough,* BREC AS BREUER *storms out just as*
DUCK AS KANDINSKY *arrives.*)

ELLIS AS MEYER: The work we do
Nurtures the collective
And brings to life
The dreams of the masses

(DUCK AS KANDINSKY *sees* KAI AS HESSE *and approaches him.)*

DUCK AS KANDINSKY: Bauhaus full of Bolshevik!

KAI AS HESSE: That's always the rumor, but it's never proven true.

DUCK AS KANDINSKY: I am serious. Communist cell in 1927 only seven students, now thirty-six!

KAI AS HESSE: The Bauhaus is abstemiously apolitical!

DUCK AS KANDINSKY: Under Gropius. Meyer allows it, encourages Bolshevism!

KAI AS HESSE: This is disturbing news, but the first I've heard of it.

DUCK AS KANDINSKY: Ask Herbert Bayer, Marcel Breuer, Laszlo Moholy-Nagy, Oskar Schlemmer. Oh, no, you can't, too late. Already resign! Klee and I resign at the end of the summer vacation if Meyer remain director.

(BREC AS STOLZL, *eating something, joins* OWEN AS KLEE *watching the speech.)*

ELLIS AS MEYER: Art is not decoration
Art is not for dramatic effect
Art is simply order
Art may serve the state
As long as the state serves the people

DUCK AS KANDINSKY: He reduce art to organization! Tidiness! International communism!

KAI AS HESSE: I can't tell you how difficult it was to get the city council to vote for extension of the Bauhaus contract. So many right-wingers now. They wouldn't have voted a pfennig for a school led by a communist!

(*Lights fade on* BREC AS STOLZL *and* OWEN AS KLEE.)

ELLIS AS MEYER: In today's world we expect art
To be fair and open to everyone,
Transformed from an individual profession
To a collective call for order

KAI AS HESSE: Director Meyer, a saving virtue of
the school has been its lack of politics. What is your
position on the continuum from communist to national
socialist?

ELLIS AS MEYER: Lord Mayor, surely you know I've
always been a theoretical Marxist! *(Returns to his speech)*
The Bauhaus henceforward rejects
The apelike excitability called talent,
Reviles scholarly sectarianism
Navel-gazing, solipsism, isolation and a fortress
mentality.

KAI AS HESSE: With all due respect, Herr Meyer, I'm
taking over momentarily.

ELLIS AS MEYER: Finishing my speech?

KAI AS HESSE: They've asked me to find a new Director
for the Bauhaus.

ELLIS AS MEYER: You found *me*!

KAI AS HESSE: But you're a communist! You hid your
views!

(KAI AS HESSE *and* DUCK AS KANDINSKY *escort* ELLIS AS
MEYER *from the stage.* HESSE *takes the rolled plans from*
MEYER.)

ELLIS AS MEYER: Kandinsky, what are you doing? This
is absurd! Hesse, let go of me! I can't believe you're
party to this outrage!

(DUCK AS KANDINSKY *disappears with* ELLIS AS MEYER.
*There may even be the sound of a thump to signal that he'll
be speaking no more.)*

KAI AS HESSE: Oh dear. *(Glances at the rolled plans)* This wasn't supposed to happen. Suddenly I'm narrating. But not for long. Hannes Mayer left Germany immediately for Moscow where he started the Red Bauhaus, confirming what everyone had feared. Gropius had no interest in stepping back into his old role as Director, so we tapped another architect, Ludwig Mies van de Rohe, best known in 1929 for his design of the German Pavilion at the International Exposition in Barcelona.

(BREC AS LUDWIG MIES VAN DER ROHE *appears in light, impeccably tailored in an elegant long coat but somewhat overweight.)*

KAI AS HESSE: He was equally well known for the furnishings of the German Pavilion, including—don't mention this to Gropius—the Barcelona Chair.

(Lights up on a Barcelona Chair. BREC AS MIES VAN DER ROHE *sits in the chair a bit grandly.)*

KAI AS HESSE: Most importantly, Mies was disinterested in politics, which meant he was acceptable to the city council in Dessau and well positioned to balance forces of the left and the right both within and without the school.

BREC AS MIES VAN DER ROHE: *(Bass voice, hands on hips)* Many believe our problem is the human situation today, but that is not a problem architecture can solve.

KAI AS HESSE: I am pleased to pass my narrative duties on to the new Director.

(KAI *as* HESSE *give the rolled plans to* BREC AS MIES VAN DER ROHE, *who stands.)*

BREC AS MIES VAN DER ROHE: Students can be shown how to work, they can be taught technique, how to reason, develop a sense of proportion, order. You can help them reach their potential, which is different for each. But the potential is not the responsibility of the teacher. Some students cannot be taught.

(ELLIS AS ERTL *rushes in.*)

ELLIS AS ERTL: Herr Director, the Communist students have taken over the canteen!

BREC AS MIES VAN DER ROHE: Are they protesting me or the firing of Hannes Meyer?

ELLIS AS ERTL: Both! It's turning into a riot! They're demanding you exhibit your work to demonstrate your fitness for office.

BREC AS MIES VAN DER ROHE: Unlikely.

ELLIS AS ERTL: And that you come down from your office and speak to them.

BREC AS MIES VAN DER ROHE: Also unlikely. Unless they disperse immediately, I will call the police to clear the canteen.

ELLIS AS ERTL: *(Delighted)* I'll tell those filthy commies! *(Runs out)*

BREC AS MIES VAN DER ROHE: The students held the canteen until the police took them away.

(KAI AS HESSE *appears.*)

KAI AS HESSE: Herr Director, I'm so sorry this disturbance inaugurates your tenure.

BREC AS MIES VAN DER ROHE: Unsurprising.

KAI AS HESSE: By official order, I'm closing the Bauhaus until you develop a plan for addressing the issue.

BREC AS MIES VAN DER ROHE: Thank you, Lord Mayor. I already have a plan. I'm expelling the entire student body.

(KAI AS HESSE *disappears and* ELLIS AS ERTL *appears before* BREC AS MIES VAN DER ROHE.*)

ELLIS AS ERTL: I must interview with you for readmission?

BREC AS MIES VAN DER ROHE: As must every student. Please sit down.

(They do. Silence as BREC AS MIES VAN DER ROHE *regards* ELLIS AS ERTL, *making him nervous.)*

ELLIS AS ERTL: *(Finally can't stand it)* Herr Director, is it no longer right to seek beauty in architecture?

BREC AS MIES VAN DER ROHE: Herr— *(Regards paper)*

ELLIS AS ERTL: Ertl!

BREC AS MIES VAN DER ROHE: Ertl.

ELLIS AS ERTL: Fritz Ertl.

BREC AS MIES VAN DER ROHE: If you are introduced to twin sisters—

ELLIS AS ERTL: Identical or fraternal?

BREC AS MIES VAN DER ROHE: In the same measure full of health, mental acuity, and financial security, and both capable of bearing children.

ELLIS AS ERTL: Yes?

BREC AS MIES VAN DER ROHE: One is homely and the other quite lovely. Which would you make your bride?

ELLIS AS ERTL: So in architecture we must choose both utility and beauty?

BREC AS MIES VAN DER ROHE: One does not preclude the other if properly designed.

ELLIS AS ERTL: And what is your commitment to group process for the development of architecture?

BREC AS MIES VAN DER ROHE: If you decide to have a baby, do you invite the neighbors to help?

ELLIS AS ERTL: I understand.

BREC AS MIES VAN DER ROHE: Good. I am requiring all returning students to sign this. *(Hands paper)*

ELLIS AS ERTL: So I am accepted for readmission?

BREC AS MIES VAN DER ROHE: Read the declaration first. If you agree to sign, you'll be admitted.

ELLIS AS ERTL: *(Scans quickly then reads)* By signing this declaration, I commit to regular course attendance, to leave the canteen as soon as my meal is consumed, to abstain from political discourse, to behave peaceably in town and to appear in public well dressed.

BREC AS MIES VAN DER ROHE: You hesitate?

ELLIS AS ERTL: No! It's just that—a number of students are political—

BREC AS MIES VAN DER ROHE: A number of students are not returning.

ELLIS AS ERTL: The communists published an article arguing that Kandinsky's introductory course is pure formalism and abstract, non-functional and based on corrugated cardboard and chicken wire.

BREC AS MIES VAN DER ROHE: I've made the introductory course optional. If the communists limit their own education, they have every right to remain stupid.

ELLIS AS ERTL: I'm no communist!

BREC AS MIES VAN DER ROHE: No politics of any kind?

(After a moment, ELLIS AS ERTL signs.)

ELLIS AS ERTL: What about faculty?

BREC AS MIES VAN DER ROHE: I know of no firebrands.

ELLIS AS ERTL: Gunta Stolzl's husband is a socialist.

BREC AS MIES VAN DER ROHE: And a Jew.

ELLIS AS ERTL: Yes.

BREC AS MIES VAN DER ROHE: Do the students whisper of such things?

ELLIS AS ERTL: Some.

BREC AS MIES VAN DER ROHE: I will not put you in the uncomfortable position of telling me their names.

ELLIS AS ERTL: Thank you.

(Lights out on ELLIS AS ERTL.*)*

BREC AS MIES VAN DER ROHE: I have my eye on that one. *(Looks at paper)* Fritz Ertl. *(Lecturing to a class)* Beauty. It is mathematics, proportions pleasing to the eye because of the arithmetic in our bones, the formulas of nature. Charlemagne's chapel at Aachen is thirty three meters high, an octagon embraced by a polygon of sixteen sides. One measurement is doubled or halved throughout, to powerful effect. It is perfection. Modern architecture, with new engineering and new materials, has the opportunity and responsibility to meet the human need for beauty as well as function. Your work must also be perfect. If I hand you back your drawing covered in black marks, do not cringe at the corrections. Simply fix it.

(Before our eyes, BREC *puts down the rolled plans and changes from* MIES VAN DER ROHE *to* GUNTA STOLZL. STOLZL *is soon joined by* ELLIS AS BERGER.*)*

BREC AS STOLZL: *(Reading a letter)* With this letter I give notice that I am stepping down from my position as an employee of the city of Dessau, effective three months from today. Negotiations about my employment at the Bauhaus may continue, however, with the prior guarantee that my status as Master of the Weaving Workshop is to be governed by a legal, long-term contract. My expectation is that my salary will be the same as that of the other Masters. Most sincerely, Gunta Stolzl.

ELLIS AS BERGER: Gunta, are you sure? It's very bold.

BREC AS STOLZL: For a woman in 1929 to expect the same pay as a man?

ELLIS AS BERGER: At least you have the title!

BREC AS STOLZL: An insult without the pay!

ELLIS AS BERGER: We must be very careful these days, Gunta.

BREC AS STOLZL: If I don't get the raise, Arieh and I are going to Moscow.

ELLIS AS BERGER: Following Meyer?

BREC AS STOLZL: I would like to see the Red Bauhaus there, but also museums, the film academy—maybe stay as long as a year—

ELLIS AS BERGER: It might be difficult for you and your Jewish husband to get back into Germany by then.

BREC AS STOLZL: In that case why would I want to come back?

ELLIS AS BERGER: You're German!

BREC AS STOLZL: My German background means almost nothing to me. I'm interested in human beings, not Germans!

ELLIS AS BERGER: They say the National Socialists will have candidates in next year's Dessau election.

BREC AS STOLZL: Who is they?

ELLIS AS BERGER: Fritz Ertl.

BREC AS STOLZL: Is Ertl himself running as a Nazi?

ELLIS AS BERGER: He can't! He would be expelled.

BREC AS STOLZL: Not if he wins.

ELLIS AS BERGER: Part of their platform will be to tear down the Bauhaus and burn it to ashes.

BREC AS STOLZL: Down with flat Jewish roofs!

ELLIS AS BERGER: You would not joke if you were an actual Jew instead of just married to one.

BREC AS STOLZL: I apologize, Otti. The National Socialists won't win. Even in provincial Dessau everyone thinks they're crazy.

ELLIS AS BERGER: I am thinking of emigrating to London or possibly back to Zagreb to care for my mother.

BREC AS STOLZL: You mustn't! We need every girl we can get!

ELLIS AS BERGER: Then don't you go to Moscow!

BOTH: To Moscow, to Moscow, to Moscow!

(They laugh at themselves. Lights out on ELLIS AS BERGER *and* BREC *turns back into* MIES VAN DER ROHE, *picking up the rolled plans.* DUCK AS KANDINSKY *and* OWEN AS KLEE *appear.)*

DUCK AS KANDINSKY: Herr Director, many thanks for seeing us.

BREC AS MIES VAN DER ROHE: Always a pleasure to see you, Kandinsky, Klee.

DUCK AS KANDINSKY: Maybe not so pleasing today.

BREC AS MIES VAN DER ROHE: Then to the point quickly. Let's get the unpleasantness over with.

*(*DUCK AS KANDINSKY *looks to* OWEN AS KLEE, *who shrugs and fills his pipe from a tobacco can.)*

DUCK AS KANDINSKY: Bauhaus is no politic.

BREC AS MIES VAN DER ROHE: I am aware of why Hannes Meyer was let go. I myself expelled the communist students.

DUCK AS KANDINSKY: But what of faculty?

BREC AS MIES VAN DER ROHE: Has someone called you a Bolshevik again?

DUCK AS KANDINSKY: No! Not me! Gunta Stolzl.

BREC AS MIES VAN DER ROHE: You are calling Gunta a Bolshevik.

DUCK AS KANDINSKY: Students have complaint.

BREC AS MIES VAN DER ROHE: Failing students. I am aware.

DUCK AS KANDINSKY: Not only failing. Three at least.

BREC AS MIES VAN DER ROHE: Is one of them Fritz Ertl?

(DUCK AS KANDINSKY *reacts.*)

BREC AS MIES VAN DER ROHE: His name comes up a lot lately.

DUCK AS KANDINSKY: I cannot say name.

BREC AS MIES VAN DER ROHE: Kandinsky, then what am I to do about it? Anonymous rumor-mongerers have no right to destroy a fine teaching career. With great effort, I've just now secured her a raise from the Dessau city council.

DUCK AS KANDINSKY: Great effort because her husband is socialist.

BREC AS MIES VAN DER ROHE: This is starting to sound familiar. Arieh Sharon is an excellent student and will be a good architect one day.

DUCK AS KANDINSKY: In Palestine!

BREC AS MIES VAN DER ROHE: Thereby making the Bauhaus Idea an international style!

DUCK AS KANDINSKY: Like international communism!

BREC AS MIES VAN DER ROHE: Or Judaism, is that what you really mean, Kandinsky?

DUCK AS KANDINSKY: I am not anti-Semite! Some of my oldest friends—Mahler, Breuer—

OWEN AS KLEE: Schönberg.

DUCK AS KANDINSKY: *(Only a moment's discomfort)* Moholy-Nagy—! Danger is to Bauhaus, to reputation. Dessau government change, looking for bad element—!

OWEN AS KLEE: Pardon—	BREC AS MIES VAN DER ROHE: Gunta Stolzl is a workshop Master, the farthest thing from a bad element—!
OWEN AS KLEE: Pardon—	DUCK AS KANDINSKY: We must to be careful!
OWEN AS KLEE: Pardon—	BREC AS MIES VAN DER ROHE: You are asking me to be the opposite of careful!

OWEN AS KLEE: I have something to say.

DUCK AS KANDINSKY: Yes, Klee, speak!	BREC AS MIES VAN DER ROHE: Please! I wondered why you were here.

*(*OWEN AS KLEE *waits until he has their full attention then slowly and calmly reads the label of his tobacco tin.)*

OWEN AS KLEE: Brinkmann. Fine cut. One hundred grams. Dutch blend. Price, sixty pfennigs.

*(*DUCK AS KANDINSKY *and* BREC AS MIES VAN DER ROHE *smile and relax. They may even laugh.* OWEN AS KLEE *does not look at them and merely smokes his pipe. Lights out on* DUCK AS KANDINSKY *and* OWEN AS KLEE.)*

BREC AS MIES VAN DER ROHE: Gunta, the three complaining students have been identified and expelled. Our investigation revealed their complaints were petty or simply untrue. Most likely politically motivated, although we can't prove it.

(BREC *puts down the plans and becomes* STOLZL, *alternating with* MIES VAN DER ROHE *[sometimes picking up the plans, sometimes leaving them].*)

BREC AS STOLZL: I am most grateful, Herr Director. I realize expelling Master Peterhans' girlfriend must have caused you a lot of trouble, especially among the faculty.

BREC AS MIES VAN DER ROHE: It's not my business who's sleeping with whom, but it's obvious why faculty getting involved with students is a bad idea.

BREC AS STOLZL: Are you referring to me, marrying Arieh? Would it be helpful to you if I simply resigned? At great effort you've gotten me a raise and now I've become a controversial figure through no action of my own—other than falling in love with a Jew—

BREC AS MIES VAN DER ROHE: (*Picking up the plans*) Gunta, please! You're an outstanding Master and a leader here at the Bauhaus for many years. It would do me no good for you to resign, only send a message to students and faculty that we tailor our policies to the politics of the moment. That we accommodate the National Socialists in a small thing—not that your role here is small—but once we let them tell us whom to hire and fire, where would it stop? Expelling all the Jewish students? Firing abstract painters? Designing only textiles with swastikas? They are not in power here in Dessau and we can still vote!

(KAI AS HESSE *appears.*)

BREC AS MIES VAN DER ROHE: Lord Mayor, when you come to see me in person, especially unannounced, I expect the worst.

KAI AS HESSE: Herr Director, I hope you don't always see me as the harbinger of doom!

BREC AS MIES VAN DER ROHE: Apologies. It's been a difficult week.

KAI AS HESSE: I am, however, about to make it more difficult.

(BREC AS MIES VAN DER ROHE *sighs.*)

KAI AS HESSE: Some of the candidates for town council are demanding an exhibition of Bauhaus projects—

BREC AS MIES VAN DER ROHE: This is starting to sound familiar.

KAI AS HESSE: Yes, I know.

BREC AS MIES VAN DER ROHE: Gropius had to mount an exhibition in Weimar in 1923.

KAI AS HESSE: And it was a triumph, acclaimed!

BREC AS MIES VAN DER ROHE: But the Thuringians still shut down the Bauhaus.

KAI AS HESSE: They're only candidates at this point.

BREC AS MIES VAN DER ROHE: Emil Evers is running against you for Mayor.

KAI AS HESSE: He has a lot of support.

BREC AS MIES VAN DER ROHE: By asking me for an exhibition, are you trying to curry favor with the conservatives in advance of the election?

KAI AS HESSE: With all due respect, I'm trying to save the Bauhaus!

BREC AS MIES VAN DER ROHE: And what should I exhibit? Conservative table lamps? National Socialist spoons?

KAI AS HESSE: Innocuous objects! Surely you have plenty of non-political product lines.

BREC AS MIES VAN DER ROHE: But you see, Lord Mayor, the Bauhaus is modern. Our designs sleek, spare, simple and beautifully utilitarian. Modern! The Nazis like Nineteenth-Century sentimental, ornamented *tchochkes*! I'm sorry, did I speak Yiddish just now? I mean baubles, trinkets, curios! The Nazis have made the modern world the enemy, frightened everyone of the future, of foreigners like Russians, Jews, Hungarians. They've made our elegant forks and spoons into crude hammers and sickles!

KAI AS HESSE: I am responsible for the Bauhaus coming to Dessau, so I feel responsible for its continued existence. I shudder to ask for this exhibition, but I believe it's the only way.

BREC AS MIES VAN DER ROHE: May it include paintings?

KAI AS HESSE: As long as people can tell what they depict.

BREC AS MIES VAN DER ROHE: That rules out Klee and Kandinsky.

KAI AS HESSE: Dear God, Kandinsky!

(*Lights out on* KAI AS HESSE *and up on* DUCK AS KANDINSKY, *who is showing* BREC AS MIES VAN DER ROHE *some paintings, perhaps projected images.*)

BREC AS MIES VAN DER ROHE: Beautiful.

DUCK AS KANDINSKY: Is called *Capricious*.

BREC AS MIES VAN DER ROHE: Perfect name. What else?

DUCK AS KANDINSKY: (*Shows another*) *Green Emptiness*.

BREC AS MIES VAN DER ROHE: Stunning. More.

DUCK AS KANDINSKY: (*Shows another*) *Three Rectangles*.

BREC AS MIES VAN DER ROHE: (*Laughs*) Three? There are at least ten!

DUCK AS KANDINSKY: Exactly! That is hint of spiritual meaning.

BREC AS MIES VAN DER ROHE: Do you have any less…?

DUCK AS KANDINSKY: Abstract?

BREC AS MIES VAN DER ROHE: You understand what we must do with this exhibition, Kandinsky?

DUCK AS KANDINSKY: You want a fishie and a moo-cow?

BREC AS MIES VAN DER ROHE: If I did, I'd ask Klee.

DUCK AS KANDINSKY: Too bad he has already resigned.

BREC AS MIES VAN DER ROHE: Yes, too bad. The National Socialists labelled him a Galician Jew.

DUCK AS KANDINSKY: He is not Jew!

BREC AS MIES VAN DER ROHE: His art looks Jewish to them because they don't understand it.

DUCK AS KANDINSKY: You would like me to show painting from 1908?

BREC AS MIES VAN DER ROHE: No—

DUCK AS KANDINSKY: 1894? I was not yet painter, but as attorney but I make doodle on subpoena.

BREC AS MIES VAN DER ROHE: Maybe the rectangles. Everybody understands rectangles.

DUCK AS KANDINSKY: And perhaps Nazis cannot count to ten.

BREC AS MIES VAN DER ROHE: Counting is what they do best. They've counted the Jewish students in the Bauhaus.

DUCK AS KANDINSKY: Seventeen. Almost every one a Communist.

BREC AS MIES VAN DER ROHE: Sometimes, Kandinsky, you sound like one of them.

DUCK AS KANDINSKY: I am no Nazi!

BREC AS MIES VAN DER ROHE: But when you warn me of Gunta Stolzl marrying a socialist—

DUCK AS KANDINSKY: Which she do!

BREC AS MIES VAN DER ROHE: We mustn't fight among ourselves. That's how they win. Nor do I wish to accommodate—

DUCK AS KANDINSKY: I will not be censor!

BREC AS MIES VAN DER ROHE: But the Lord Mayor believes we can only save our jobs by exhibiting acceptable chairs, chess sets, tableware—

DUCK AS KANDINSKY: And no painting by Kandinsky?! With Klee gone, I am most famous artist in Bauhaus. With no Kandinsky, exhibition will be weird.

BREC AS MIES VAN DER ROHE: They're sending Paul Schultze-Naumberg to render his artistic judgment.

DUCK AS KANDINSKY: Schultze-Naumberg?! Asshole architect who write *Art and Race*?

BREC AS MIES VAN DER ROHE: Yes, the fellow who destroyed Schlemmer's mural in the Weimar Bauhaus last year.

DUCK AS KANDINSKY: He say abstract art come from race-mixing!

BREC AS MIES VAN DER ROHE: Is *Three Rectangles* the work of a racially mixed artist?

DUCK AS KANDINSKY: Am pure Russian!

BREC AS MIES VAN DER ROHE: But vulnerably abstract.

DUCK AS KANDINSKY: Maybe not painting then.

BREC AS MIES VAN DER ROHE: Thank you for understanding.

DUCK AS KANDINSKY: *(Thrusting a document toward* BREC AS MIES VAN DER ROHE*)* Show analysis instead.

BREC AS MIES VAN DER ROHE: *(Examining it)* What's this?

DUCK AS KANDINSKY: Analysis of abstract painting. Intellectual explication clear enough for Nazi to understand. Transparent!

BREC AS MIES VAN DER ROHE: Intellectual? That's exactly what we don't need!

DUCK AS KANDINSKY: You need Kandinsky!

(DUCK AS KANDINSKY *grabs the paper and smacks it down on a table. Lights out on* DUCK AS KANDINSKY *and up on* KAI AS HESSE, ELLIS AS ERTL *and* OWEN AS SCHULTZE-NAUMBERG, *a fat, elderly man with glasses, a Nazi medal and a droopy mustache.* ERTL *and* SCHULTZE-NAUMBERG *wear swastika armbands.)*

BREC AS MIES VAN DER ROHE: Doctor Schultze-Naumberg, welcome.

OWEN AS SCHULTZE-NAUMBERG: *(Nasal)* Mies Van Der Rohe, a pleasure to meet you at last.

BREC AS MIES VAN DER ROHE: I hope you'll enjoy our small exhibition. We're very proud of the work.

KAI AS HESSE: All of Dessau is proud of the Bauhaus.

OWEN AS SCHULTZE-NAUMBERG: It looks rather like the housewares department of Karstadt Warenhaus.

BREC AS MIES VAN DER ROHE: The Bauhaus has partnered with industry to create beauty in utility for the German people.

OWEN AS SCHULTZE-NAUMBERG: Have you anything by your most famous artist?

BREC AS MIES VAN DER ROHE: Paul Klee is no longer with the Bauhaus.

OWEN AS SCHULTZE-NAUMBERG: Wassily Kandinsky.

(BREC AS MIES VAN DER ROHE *surreptitiously removes the analysis from the table and steers them away from it.*)

BREC AS MIES VAN DER ROHE: Oh, we must have something of his over here on the wall.

OWEN AS SCHULTZE-NAUMBERG: *(Perusing the wall display)* No…no…ah.

BREC AS MIES VAN DER ROHE: From our textile workshop. A simple pattern derived from traditional Teutonic weaves.

OWEN AS SCHULTZE-NAUMBERG: Ah. Ah. Oh.

BREC AS MIES VAN DER ROHE: That's a Moholy-Nagy photogram.

OWEN AS SCHULTZE-NAUMBERG: X-rays as art? What's the front? What's the back?

BREC AS MIES VAN DER ROHE: Yes, he wants us to see through objects we think of as solid. He calls it the New Vision, a way to see more than the eye can perceive.

OWEN AS SCHULTZE-NAUMBERG: Modern nonsense!

BREC AS MIES VAN DER ROHE: It's a Renaissance idea, rather like pentimento in a painting or a palimpsest on vellum, you can see the past and present simultaneously.

OWEN AS SCHULTZE-NAUMBERG: *(Snorts)* He's one of your foreign instructors. Hungarian?

BREC AS MIES VAN DER ROHE: He left in 1928 to start his own studio in Berlin.

OWEN AS SCHULTZE-NAUMBERG: I see no Kandinsky.

BREC AS MIES VAN DER ROHE: I'm almost certain he submitted something.

OWEN AS SCHULTZE-NAUMBERG: Perhaps so abstract we can't even recognize it as a painting!

BREC AS MIES VAN DER ROHE: Kandinsky's done many realistic works as well.

OWEN AS SCHULTZE-NAUMBERG: Recently?

BREC AS MIES VAN DER ROHE: Certainly! I could have sworn—

OWEN AS SCHULTZE-NAUMBERG: Herr Director, as much as I'm enjoying this display, I do have serious business with you.

BREC AS MIES VAN DER ROHE: Our exhibition is serious business indeed.

OWEN AS SCHULTZE-NAUMBERG: I'm talking about Bauhaus pedagogy.

BREC AS MIES VAN DER ROHE: I'd be delighted to show you our course catalogue.

OWEN AS SCHULTZE-NAUMBERG: That will not be necessary. *(With a glance at* ERTL*)* I understand three students have been expelled for filing a complaint against a teacher.

BREC AS MIES VAN DER ROHE: Their complaints were investigated and found to be baseless. Blatant lies and false attacks. The offenders were rejected by the student body and then officially.

OWEN AS SCHULTZE-NAUMBERG: By you.

BREC AS MIES VAN DER ROHE: By me. I am the Director. Discipline is ultimately my responsibility.

OWEN AS SCHULTZE-NAUMBERG: I am reinstating those students.

BREC AS MIES VAN DER ROHE: By what authority?

OWEN AS SCHULTZE-NAUMBERG: I apologize. I have no official authority over the Bauhaus at the moment. But

I kindly suggest that the Dessau City Council would be pleased to know those students were re-admitted. Especially after next week's elections.

(*Lights out on everyone but* BREC AS MIES VAN DER ROHE.)

BREC AS MIES VAN DER ROHE: My dear Gunta. I can hardly speak I am so angry and disgusted. But the matter has become existential for the Bauhaus. I am distressed to take you up on your offer to resign.

(BREC AS MIES VAN DER ROHE *puts a green envelope and the rolled plans on the table.* BREC *becomes* STOLZL *and picks up the envelope.*)

BREC AS STOLZL: I am easily replaced, perhaps with Lily Reich, or Otti Berger were she not a Jew. But as you yourself said, if you do not stand up to tiny tyrants, your acquiescence feeds them and they grow. Still ridiculous, still petty, still unreasonable, but now so big they eat you.

(*Alternating between* MIES VAN DER ROHE *and* STOLZL, BREC *touches or picks up either the green envelope or plans.*)

BREC AS MIES VAN DER ROHE: I will not let them eat the Bauhaus.

BREC AS STOLZL: They may eat more than that. Perhaps someday I will thank you for saving the Bauhaus even though it means sacrificing me. I understand this isn't really your decision, but you do have a choice and so do I.

BREC AS MIES VAN DER ROHE: We are part of Dessau, part of the community. When the community rejects us, the Bauhaus is no more. Remember what happened to Gropius, to Meyer. I am responsible for the entire school!

BREC AS STOLZL: (*Opens the green envelope, reads letter inside*) Thank you, Herr Director. You've been very generous to me under the circumstances. I shall be pleased to escape the intrigues and back-biting. Our friendly Bauhaus world is tearing itself apart without and within. Perhaps the school is no longer worth saving.

(BREC AS STOLZL *turns away to leave.* KAI AS HESSE *arrives, and* BREC *picks up the plans and turns around, now as* MIES VAN DER ROHE.)

KAI AS HESSE: Ludwig, it's most regrettable that I must disturb you.

BREC AS MIES VAN DER ROHE: I've been waiting for you since the elections.

KAI AS HESSE: I am still Mayor, but almost the entire council is National Socialist. Soon they will send me packing as well, I'm sure.

BREC AS MIES VAN DER ROHE: I'm sorry. You've been our hero.

KAI AS HESSE: The new council has already signaled its intention to cut off funding for the Bauhaus.

BREC AS MIES VAN DER ROHE: Unsurprising.

KAI AS HESSE: They even want to tear down the buildings, to erase any memory, burn them to ashes. Before I'm out of office, I can allocate some emergency funds—

BREC AS MIES VAN DER ROHE: No need, Lord Mayor. Our licensing and patents as well as direct sale of Bauhaus products have grown as quickly in recent months as the antipathy of Dessau.

BREC AS MIES VAN DER ROHE: We've accrued enough funds to rent a warehouse in Berlin.

KAI AS HESSE: Berlin?!

BREC AS MIES VAN DER ROHE: I'm tired of small town living, small town—smallness.

KAI AS HESSE: Do you have a fiscal sponsor in Berlin?

BREC AS MIES VAN DER ROHE: I'm taking the school independent. We make enough money now. We can afford it. Imagine, Lord Mayor, the Bauhaus answering to no one but ourselves, free!

KAI AS HESSE: Perhaps I will join you in Berlin myself!

(They shake hands.)

BREC AS MIES VAN DER ROHE: It was no empty boast. Enrollment was bursting, waiting lists of prospective students, products and designs selling left and right. The Bauhaus was at its apex when the Dessau Nazis shut us down. I found an empty telephone warehouse in Berlin, and we did what we did best: work, building, creating a new world out of nothing.

(The students become themselves.)

OWEN: Thank you for joining us for The Bauhaus Project II: Dessau.

ELLIS: Y'all might think that's the end, but we're not done.

BREC: Due to the success—I guess we can call it success—?

(The others nods and murmur assent, "definitely" "yes, success.")

BREC: The administration has asked us to finish the story of the Bauhaus.

OWEN: But very carefully.

DUCK: *Bauhaus Project Part Three: Berlin!*

KAI: We haven't agreed on a title yet—

BREC: It's a collaborative process—   DUCK: Argument! Experiment!

OWEN: Rather like the Bauhaus. Messy, undisciplined, passionate, brilliant—

DUCK: Creative.

ELLIS: But we should tell you what happened to Fritz Ertl—

OWEN: No, we shouldn't—   ELLIS: Otti Berger—

KAI: Arnold Schönberg—   BREC: Walter Gropius—

DUCK: Wassily Kandinsky!   ELLIS: Maria Kipp—

ELLIS: Alma Mahler!

OWEN: Save it for the third presentation!

ELLIS: All right, y'all come back now, y'hear?

KAI: With all due respect, I have to say—

OWEN: No, you don't—

KAI: Fuuuuuuck!

(OWEN *cedes the floor*)

KAI: I have to say I was more than skeptical about this project. Only one of us is an actor.

ELLIS: I'm not an actor. I'm a director!

KAI: We're designers, artists—

DUCK: Musicians!

KAI: But acting tricked us into—

ELLIS: Acting didn't trick you—God!   OWEN: Nobody forced anybody—

KAI: By becoming these—pioneers of design—   OWEN: It's history! It really happened!

KAI: We learned—experienced—   BREC: These humans—

ELLIS: Empathy!

KAI: Yeah, empathy. That's what you want, isn't it? For people, not heroes—

OWEN: They're still my heroes.

KAI: Flawed but still… I mean…

ELLIS: We shall see.

DUCK: Eat a bowl of fuck!

(Embarrassed silence)

OWEN: I'd like to thank my colleagues for that last—incoherent—and profane—jumble. But that's not where we shall end. Instead: a final word from Oskar Schlemmer.

(Everyone takes their places on the staircase. Bauhaus music.)

KAI AS SCHLEMMER: Although I'd fled when Hannes Meyer became Director, I was devastated two years later when I heard the Dessau Bauhaus closed. It was then I remembered the photographs I'd taken of the staircase, with eager students, artists and designers of the future, going up and down.

(An image of SCHLEMMER'S *famous Bauhaustreppe painting appears, almost a mirror of the real staircase and the students on it, with only a few differences.)*

KAI AS SCHLEMMER: I quickly painted from the photographs and from memory, in case the Nazis carried out their threat to destroy the beautiful modern home Gropius built for us in Dessau. It was my way of saying farewell to the Bauhaus, so all the figures—except my own—face away, ascending.

(KAI AS SCHLEMMER joins them on the staircase and everyone adjusts their pose to match the painting exactly. Lights fade on the stairs. The image of the painting lasts a moment longer, then disappears.)

END OF PLAY